MW01518775

COME FROM NOWHERE

A Memoir in Two Halves

Come from Nowhere

A Memoir in Two Halves

Bian An

{ Ann Bennett Spence }

LUMINARE PRESS

WWW.LUMINAREPRESS.COM

Printed in the United States of America

Photography by Josiah W. Bennett
Cover Design by Claire Flint Last

Luminare Press
442 Charnelton St.
Eugene, OR 97401
www.luminarepress.com

LCCN: 2022916425
ISBN: 979-8-88679-171-6

To my parents
Josiah Whitney Bennett and Zhou Nianci
Who were stricken too young

"The death of a second parent is like the disappearance of a planet from the sky. It has vanished, with its religion, its customs, its own peculiar habits and rituals."

—*Gabriel Garcia Marquez*

CONTENTS

EPILOGUE

PREFACE

Where are you from? Not a question I can ever answer easily. I could say Washington DC and be done with it. But that would be false. Or I could say Exeter. Or China. Or nowhere in particular.

My childhood was spent half in America and half abroad. This memoir springs half from America and half from China.

The half in America was episodic, but it had a through-line that was New Hampshire, the Exeter/Hampton area. That's where my grandparents had a house, my American grandparents. Every summer possible, my sister and I stayed with them, briefly or not. Until college, this area was my surest grasp of America. Later I learned that my father had given free rein to his demons—his thirst for adventure—in the mountains of New Hampshire and beyond until he left for Beijing during the Japanese invasion of China.

If my American grandparents seem to loom large in my memory, it's because my father's family—my American family—was all the family I had. The Chinese half, my mother's family, was torn away at the root, my Chinese grandfather killed in Beijing by Japanese soldiers before I was born, my grandmother unreachable through to her death during the Cultural Revolution. Yet China was where I started in life; it's my first memories, my first language, and the imprint that led me toward how I've lived my adult life.

Half this, half that, is the story of my life. The first half of this memoir locates itself right here in Exeter and the sliver of New Hampshire coastline that's Hampton and Rye. The second half veers into the mysteries of my main childhood, starting in China. It's the Chinese civil war and the Cold War that drive my young years. The Vietnam War comes later, by stealth first and then by blast.

I write from memory as best I recall. And I write as Ann Bennett Spence, by which name I've been known—but also as *Bian An,* my Chinese name from birth.

Bian An
Ann Bennett Spence
Exeter, New Hampshire
2023

Exeter, New Hampshire, America

Throughline

P *ut on your shoes—we're going to Exeter. No flip-flops.*
This is serious. My grandmother speaking. She lived
in Hampton, where nothing was serious except the
odd family ghost.

We'd visit my grandparents in New Hampshire every
summer we could—my sister and I, along with our parents
on home leave from foreign shores. After my grandfather went
from retirement straight to his grave, it was just Grandma in
Hampton. She was practically an institution, someone who'd
go on forever, we thought, in her loving eccentricities. She
took us to Exeter when there was serious business to be done.
The bank. The lawyer. The store where we bought a record
player for $50, which was serious money in 1963.

Even more serious was Phillips Exeter Academy, where
there were lots of boys who were bound for the big time, I
was told. Big Time meant Harvard in those days. William
Saltonstall, he of the impossibly bushy eyebrows and open
manner, headed the school and held his front door open
wide whenever my family visited, which was often. Later
our paths crossed in Nigeria, but that's another story.

Also later, in college, my heart was broken by one of
those bound-for-glory Exeter boys who'd landed at Harvard

so articulate and witty that he'd stir wild laughter even from flat-lined conversation, and pull roars from audiences at the Hasty Pudding Show that he co-headed. Vietnam put an end to his laughter. And by Vietnam I mean the war that we call the Vietnam War while the Vietnamese call it the American War. He never came back from that war, not really. But that's yet another story.

I grew up without a home town: my father was in the Foreign Service, and so my family moved about every two years, starting in China, and then Taiwan, Israel, Nigeria, and South Vietnam in that order. But nothing was orderly. We were surrounded by war, or recent war, or soon-to-be war, wherever we went. No dainty postings in Europe, no top hats to greet the Queen at the Court of St. James, no frills, no prestige. Just no nonsense, and sometimes old army jeeps for transportation. Wherever we went, we spoke nostalgically, nay reverentially of "The States," where the streets were always clean and shining, where there weren't any bombed-out ruins nor sewage in the open, and you could get real milk, not just the powdered kind. And ice cream.

Ask me my happiest memory of New Hampshire summers, and I'll tell you it was when we piled into the back of the station wagon and were driven to the ice cream stand in Greenland. We were kids. The ice cream stand was the main thing in Greenland, not far from Exeter and Hampton. On summer nights, during the drive you could almost hear the bugs splatting on the windshield and see fireflies everywhere. Back in the back, we slurped our ice cream. On the radio, which was controlled by the grownups, we'd hear *Where Are You, Little Star?* by The Elegants. It was heaven.

Bian An (Ann Bennett Spence)

So very far it was, this throughline, from the random, off-color, off-kilter, noisy, jolting, and always strange stuff of our ordinary lives when not in The States. Not-in-The-States. And strange could be monstrous or sweet but never could it be safely stored away. It could bite, and not just in nightmares.

1. Color

"Why Nancy, you're brown as a *berry!*" Grandma again, with a frown.

"Oh. That's just from waterskiing all the time, Tarkwa Beach—Lagos." My mother speaking, with a conciliatory laugh.

"Well." A pause. "I should say, you're not in Lagos now." A twist of her pursed lips, and my grandmother picks up her leather handbag and heads for the door. "I'm off to Exeter." Businesslike and dismissive.

A shrug from my mother, and then a merry wave of her brown arm, "Have a good time!" she calls out, and I hear mischief in her tone.

No response from my grandmother as she marches off to the car, sensible shoes, sensible purse held rigidly, body language signaling annoyance. Was there *ever* a "good time" to be had in Exeter? Exeter was business!

Always, as soon as my grandmother turned onto North Shore Road and drove away toward Exeter, my mother would open the refrigerator to sniff the many individual containers of leftovers. Were it up to her, the leftovers would never have been sitting there on the shelves; they'd have disappeared the very next night, disguised as some Chinese dish with a name made up by my mother but always savory and always gulped down approvingly by family. But my grandmother didn't believe in mixing things—after all, the green beans were the green beans, and the carrots were the carrots—forever separated, unto their death by mold. And thus my mother would throw out moldy leftovers, dribs and drabs, shaking her head over the waste of it all. "Don't tell Grandma," she'd say conspiratorially, and my grandmother would never notice. Or never remark, if she did notice.

My mother was Chinese, and let's face it, my grandmother didn't like it when her daughter-in-law got "too brown." Probably even after a quarter century my grandparents couldn't believe that their son and firstborn had brought a "Chinese girl" into their very Republican household. Married her practically right off the boat from Shanghai, in the popular imagination of that time. But actually my mother was college-educated, absolutely fluent in English, and utterly charming when she wanted to be, which was usually. She always wore a *qipao* (a "Suzie Wong" dress), a slim fit with side slits to show off the legs she was so proud of. For parties the dress was silk, worn with jade and gold necklace and earrings. For daytime the dress was cotton, worn plain and striking. But the dress was never sensible, according to my grandmother. And the subtext was that it was too Chinese.

When my mother walked into the restaurant, Pier Four on the Boston harbor, I remember the look in my date's eyes. Astonished. Gobsmacked. Afterwards he remarked to me, *She's really Chinese,* as though I hadn't made it clear that my mother is Chinese. You see, I don't "look Chinese"—no almond eyes, no black hair or whatever other racial traits they expect—so people discount the Chinese in me, to their regret, and to mine. That was the last time I saw that date, the one who then graduated from Harvard and went off to Vietnam, U.S. Army, ground warfare, bad outcome.

Color came up often. A year after college, at age 22, I was still learning color—not as in art, or fashion, or fall foliage. As in classification by race.

My fiancé and I were applying for a marriage license at City Hall in Cambridge, Massachusetts, an immense Romanesque stone building with a central tower and noisy air conditioners sticking out of the windows. Marriage licenses were issued in an office inside to the left of the front door. At the counter, the clerk looked bored and oppressed by the heat. She handed us each a form and told us to fill them out.

The forms were simple enough, until I got to the part that required me to check a box to indicate my color. The options presented were white, black, red, and yellow.

"My mother's Chinese," I said. No need to say that my father's white, since I look all-white. "So I'm half white, half Chinese."

The clerk looked at me, narrowed her eyes and said nothing, possibly thinking I was joking.

"I'll check both the white box and the yellow box, okay?" I asked, thinking that's the obvious thing to do.

Suddenly she focused on the form, then zeroed in on me coldly and snapped, "No Dearie, you can't do that, not at all, you have to choose *one*. Or *the other*." Her smudgy index finger pressed down hard, first on the white box and then on the yellow box. By then she'd gone into full huff, hands on her hips and glaring. Perhaps daring me.

I chose yellow: *the other.*

Later I told people I was more annoyed about being called "Dearie" than about being pushed to choose. But that's not true. Being shoved into the yellow box or the white box was what grated—because neither box contains the truth.

TODAY I DRIVE ACROSS THE ACADEMY, EXETER, SEVERAL times a week. I stop obediently at the two campus pedestrian crossings and watch as backpacked kids, now coed and multicolored, rush or amble across the street, some waving politely to the stopped traffic. I can't connect these kids to the intensity of the Exeter boy—no, the man—I once knew. Maybe he was intense, living intensely, because he'd had to deal with the draft. The draft menaced young manhood everywhere in this country, and it attacked just beyond the bend in the road ahead, the beyond you can't see until it's too late. It killed. It often maimed the mind if not the body. Some escaped it with faked excuses, some ran toward the danger, some were caught off-guard or found safe quarter, and some simply got seized by the undertow, dragged to perdition. I think: none of these kids today have to deal with the draft.

But scot-free they're not. Thus my mind goes to *A Separate Peace,* the novel that spoke to me first because it was about supposed peace at Exeter the Academy in the midst of World War II, not unlike supposed peace in the U.S. in the midst of the war in Vietnam. Later the novel spoke to me as a story of rivalry and impetuous actions. Schoolboys who suddenly grew up. But switch the main characters and have the jostler be the one who dies, while the one who lives is unaware for decades, unaware of what happened.

2. Out of the Blue

Car accidents come out of nowhere. The one that took a friend's life happened in Italy, a shock that reverberates today, despite (or because of) my being barely 24 at that time. It stunned me. It stunned all who knew her. She was only 23, a young mother.

Another car accident, far less consequential, had happened over six years earlier on one of the winding country backroads around Exeter, somewhere near Drinkwater Road. It was just before I started college. A friend was behind the wheel, and she and I were bound for her house with a salad I'd prepared for lunch there. There was light drizzle, and rock 'n roll radio dominated the slap-slap of windshield wipers. On my right, out of nowhere a utility truck backed into the front end of our car. In the flash before impact I slammed my upper body onto the seat beside me (no seatbelts and no bucket seats back then), so the truck's protruding lumber load went over my head. Glass from the shattered windshield sliced my hand. When I looked up from the seat, I saw a lettuce leaf swiping back and forth, skewered on a wiper bereft of its windshield. My friend's face was bleeding from cuts by the glass, and no doubt she'd had a concussion because she wasn't quite coherent. But we both climbed out of the car with what they'd later describe as minor bleeding from minor cuts and minor abrasions. Minor, minor, minor. The car was totaled.

My grandparents were shocked. The town hurriedly sent two officials over, to make sure I was all right, and to note my response and (perhaps more to the point) my grandparents' reaction, for liability purposes. Of course no one sued. Who'd sue for an honest mistake of no lasting damage? But my friend and I, we knew how close it had been, the glass that clipped her, and the lumber that would have obliterated my face, my head, had I not gone down fast.

At that time, my parents and younger sister were in Lagos. When they learned about the accident, my parents phoned, a rare event because international calls were very costly. Our brief, expensive, staccato conversation left them clueless about the near-miss. I showed up for my freshman year at college with my right hand in a bandage but otherwise reasonably intact. The scar on my hand, still visible even today, is a continuing reminder that when life goes along there are always alternative scenarios, near-misses you're not even aware of. You save your strength for the blows that *don't* miss, and still you forge on. I hear my mother in these words, my mother who didn't let grave losses stop her.

We were in Lagos when Mr. Saltonstall, as I called him, arrived to do damage control. At the invitation of John F. Kennedy he'd left Exeter in 1963, after nearly 20 years heading the Academy, to head the Peace Corps in Nigeria. There he found backwash from the infamous Postcard Incident in which a volunteer in the very first Peace Corps group to arrive in Nigeria wrote her negative impressions *on a postcard* no less. It was read by a Nigerian postal worker and then widely publicized in that country and worldwide. Today, when online sneering is commonplace, it's hard to understand that the incident still rankled in Nigeria two years afterwards. Bill Saltonstall was still dealing with the optics (as they now say) of a privileged white American dissing the difficult living conditions of those in a nation only just freed from colonialism.

Kennedy was assassinated not long after Saltonstall took on the Peace Corps assignment, and Saltonstall stayed only two years before retiring to a coastal town in Massachusetts to pursue his passion for sailing.

Unlike him, just before I retired, I returned to Exeter. I'd bought a condo right next to the railroad tracks, on Front Street, where the Downeaster train roaring by at 4:10 a.m. didn't even wake me up, because I'd already be awake and about to have breakfast before catching a commuter train into Boston. In June 2016, BBC radio informed me as I was pouring my coffee that Brexit had prevailed in the U.K. Carefully, I put down the coffee mug, and in that instant I knew that our world had changed. It was almost a JFK moment.

So Exeter—the town, the Academy, the memory—is complex. It crosses my mind in different guises. It's never inert. It changes.

3. Rising Water

Hampton could get complicated too, more than the honky-tonk clatter of the Casino and the spring vacation college crowds my grandparents complained about every year (*Fire Hoses Shoot Water as Teenage Crowds Rampage on the Boardwalk,* a headline might say). We kids didn't understand that stuff, and the grownups would change the subject when we asked.

North Beach, the beach that *we* knew, didn't have parties or loudness of any kind beyond the crash of surf. Not like the "Big Beach" of merry-making and casino, our beach was to be played on, dug up for sand castles and little rivers of water, walked along in search of starfish or hermit crabs. We'd get in and out of swimwear and wash sand off our feet with a hose at our ramshackle beach cottage, which still stands small among its ever-expanding neighboring homes—though no longer ramshackle, nor ours.

From the front porch of the beach cottage we'd clamber down splintery stairs to the sand, then race to the water, then downbeach to the barnacles and mussels stuck to jagged rocks, deftly skipped over at low tide. Careless about slipping or falling, we never did. Today I can't begin to address those rocks; they're a formidable barrier, not a pastime.

Only on the Fourth of July did we go to the Big Beach, with parents and grandparents steering us through the crowds, maybe stopping near the Casino to buy Buzzell's candy popcorn for us kids. At dusk we'd sit on the sand, munching the popcorn under the vigilant eyes of the grownups, waiting for the fireworks to start, past bedtime, digging our feet under the warm sand and then feeling the warmth slowly turn cold with the descent of night. And then the fireworks! Setting the dark sky ablaze with a towering wizard's flash and noise, they never disappointed us.

My grandparents' home, "the Hampton house," was a mile away from the shore, on North Beach Road, now renamed Cusack Road. It had an unobstructed view of the Atlantic Ocean, whether blue or stormy, across tidal marshes. The east wind would bring a strong scent of seaweed to our large wraparound porch, and my grandmother would always, always remark, and always with the same words and inflection: *how good to smell the ocean!* Rotting seaweed, my father would then say, and my grandmother would brush off the remark with a mere chuckle, her mischievous son not to be taken seriously. The seaweed smell was an acquired taste, friends would always say later, out of earshot from my folks.

Me, I'd look at that ocean and imagine it rising inexorably and reaching the house, rising still more, forcing us out and making us swim endlessly toward safety. Those thoughts came to me as a kid, maybe because we'd been through typhoons in Taiwan, or maybe because my father had told us scare stories about tsunamis. That mischievous son. He liked to scare his kids, thinking it was merely a shiver, when in fact it became a permanent mark. Rising water became the stuff of nightmares.

So too with the Isles of Shoals, those barren islands visible off the coast, where once there were fishermen with grit sufficient to survive punishing winters for summers of bare granite and wildflowers. My grandparents thought the islands beautiful, and we'd go by boat to Star Island for sunny picnics on rocks presided over by a mournful abandoned inn. That inn, my father would say, had tales to tell. And he'd hint at long-ago murder and madness while again my grandmother would brush away the remarks like pesky flies. Later I'd learn he was both right and wrong. Star Island is not Smuttynose, another island among the Isles of Shoals where indeed there had been dark doings some 75 years earlier.

Was it my father who'd given us to understand that his grandfather Benjamin Whitney had shot himself in the attic office of his home? Decades after the death, as children playing hide-and-go-seek at that large house now of his widow, my great-grandmother, we were always afraid of the attic, so sure we were that it was haunted. Wrong. Rewrite: official records, found more recently, say my great-grandfather died of cyanide poisoning—still "a suicide" says the record, but never mind that attic.

Then I learn from his college reunion book that before his death at 54 he'd been feeling progressively unwell, becoming uncharacteristically reclusive, and increasingly so over many years, to the consternation of his classmates. So: was it *slow* cyanide poisoning, possibly from his work as an interior designer which involved cyanide-based paints? Then throw in the everyday availability of cyanide, strychnine, and arsenic (like today's easily obtainable guns), as well as a mysterious "Uncle" Stanley, a governess, a housekeeper, and a maid, all residents at various times in that big house along with his wife and three children, my grandmother the eldest of the children. There's a story here, one among many that were perhaps deliberately muddied for us during my childhood.

You never know, my father would say. My mother would shrug as though it didn't matter, but usually it was just because you couldn't talk about it—*bukeyi,* not allowed—because my grandmother's eyes would flash irritation at any mention of the loss of the father she'd held so dear. She made certain it was never discussed.

She'd also close down any discussion of my grandfather's older brother who disappeared on his honeymoon cruise, off the coast of Italy, never to be seen again. Or of her Uncle Stephen who'd fought at the siege of Vicksburg—for the Confederacy. Her father Benjamin had been born during the siege, losing his young mother a year after his birth. The motherless youngster was partly raised by his older half-siblings, because his father, by then 57 years old and twice-widowed, was perhaps unable to cope with an infant. Was older half-brother Stephen an influence on Benjamin? Does any of this have anything to do with Benjamin's death by suicide (or not)? All we know is that despite joining the Confederacy, after its defeat Stephen returned to Massachusetts to live long and comfortably, ultimately finding eternal rest in the Whitney family plot at the most elegant cemetery of the Boston area. Though he was shunned in life by his Yankee kin who'd lost husbands and fiancés and sons to the Civil War, the family plot doesn't discriminate. Both sides of that war lie buried there. As do both sides of the Cold War, two generations later.

Back to the Hampton house. It had cedar shingles and trigger-latch doors and replicas of Renaissance paintings of baby angels and the Virgin Mary, in one of its common spaces. An enormous fieldstone fireplace had a cedar mantelpiece, above which there hung a long rifle, a horizontal mystery that no one discussed beyond saying it belonged to an ancestor. Which ancestor? Shrugs and silence.

Around the house and across the road was lots of land, or so it seemed, mostly woodland. Under rocks and pine needles near the house, a cousin and I buried a time capsule, circa 1956. When years later I tried to find it, I failed. Then the buyers of the property tore down the house for an updated look, and no doubt the time capsule was crushed by bulldozers or junked in a landfill. In memory, though, the Hampton house lives on for its frenzied activity of summer days, and its inexplicable groanings and creakings of summer nights.

My grandmother was stricken at 90 at Wentworth by the Sea, a gilded-age hotel that had gone tawdry, but still gave her the view of the ocean and sometimes the smell of seaweed she so loved. She'd been chugging along until one July, when suddenly she found she couldn't walk. By December she was gone, probably as she'd wanted to: without a fuss. Yet her loss was unbearable for me. She was the only grandmother I'd ever had, the only grandparent still living, heading the only family I knew, because after age three I was never again to see my Chinese grandmother who lived in Beijing behind that mysterious Bamboo Curtain I grew up with. And while my American grandfather had died in his 70s at a hospital in Cambridge, my Chinese grandfather had been killed in his 50s by Japanese soldiers on a street in Beijing during the Japanese occupation of that city, which my mother then fled.

In our Exeter home today, there hangs a contemporary painting of a turbulent ocean that has a concrete structure floating amidst waves. It's a critique of Brutalist architecture, or a depiction of the rising waters of climate change, or a reference to life's turbulence—or all three. It's probably political. It may be prophetic. It's definitely agitated. But beyond it, through the windows, you see calm trees clothed in sunshine.

Wheet, wheet, jub-jub-jub-jub-jub-jub is the commentary from a bird, and a small rabbit hops away, beyond vision. My mother was born in the Year of the Rabbit, and during Beijing winters in college she wore a coat of rabbit fur although not when she helped lead a student demonstration against the Japanese invaders—such a coat was too privileged. Enthusiastic about western science, she nevertheless always looked for signs, auspicious signs she'd call them. So, since her death, for me a rabbit is auspicious, a good sign, a sign of approval. That a rabbit crossed my path on the day I sent off my first manuscript, was not lost on me.

4. Randolph

A quick segue to the White Mountains, with their own majesty and mystery. When my parents left me dockside on Manhattan's west side, sailing off with my younger sister in tow, I was unmoored. A photo taken from shipboard shows me looking utterly stricken by the ship's departure. Abandoned by family. In a month I'd be starting at a tiny, obscure boarding school in upstate New York, but meanwhile at the Hampton house I looked to the ocean—quietly, sadly, pondering a ship sailing away from me, toward Africa.

So my grandparents tried to anchor me by taking me to their land in Randolph, deep in the White Mountains, facing Mt. Adams. It's where they'd regularly stayed with their children, including my father their first-born, for camping and hiking along the Appalachian Trail and the many other trails of Randolph. My father, a bit of a loner even in childhood, took to the wildness of the mountains and learned to go his own way, eventually to leave his parents wholly behind.

At Randolph my grandparents and I stayed at the Mt. Crescent House, a 19th-century hotel with a gracious front porch and what had become an elderly if prosperous clientele. I was the only youngster. I riffled through *National Geographic* magazines with photos of the huts and trails of the White Mountains; developed a teenage crush on the tanned and sweaty "hut boys" pictured hiking with hut supplies on their backs; and generally felt no less outcast, no less unmoored. A bored, anxious, too-quiet teenager.

But once we started hitting the trail, day after day hiking the Randolph land and surrounds, I found connection to something not just physical. It was something in the air, something close to my American family, the Bennetts and the Whitneys, for decades before. I lost my apprehension about a strange boarding school, only concentrating on walking: stepping through and over jagged granite, pebbly trails, across streams, in sunshine or rain, whichever prevailed. My grandparents spoke of these mountains as something almost sacred, while my father had gloried in their majestic beauty as a place for adventure, or for solitude in nature, taking solo trips to the mountains to be away from his parents.

Because Randolph mattered to my father, because he introduced it to my mother with such pride (right after she'd arrived from China), proud of its isolation and bleakness and pristine beauty, knowing she'd be astonished at what *wasn't* there: crowds of people, bold color, loud haggling, thus here in Randolph a quiet she'd never known, a place where just the two of them could be together—because of all that, I hope one day to see simply the name Bennett cut plainly into a granite boulder on the land, to mark where east met west in a union that lasted a lifetime. Two lifetimes.

5. Communists

During the McCarthy years, the television set blinked black and white, depicting Congressional hearings where pointed fingers and arcane lists would single out so-called Communists as though they were hiding under the credenza or sitting in plain sight at the dining table. My mother had an enormous extended family in so-called Red China. Thus my father, in the State Department, could attract the pointed finger just for being married to a Chinese whose entire family was in a country that had just "turned Communist." It's certain his career was held back. Yet it was also certain, for similar reasons, that my mother would never again be able to see her own family in China. Whose loss was greater? You tell me.

The irony was that the Communists were not only in China. They were in my American family too, from the get-go. My Republican grandparents' second son went to Harvard, where he became president of the student union and then later joined the American Communist Party. He ran for Congress on that ticket. He lost.

A few years earlier, on graduating, he'd become a television repairman in order to organize electrical workers, my parents said. He and his second wife—my uncle and aunt—often visited the Hampton house when we were there also, and the State Department's anti-communist protocols required that my father write up each night spent under the same roof as his Communist brother and sister-in-law. To a child, this translated as caution about my uncle. At night I imagined him tiptoeing around the house and stealthily going through my father's papers while trying not to click the trigger door latches that always woke me. Wide awake. Childishly afraid. The airwaves, that TV, were full of paranoia about Communists. And they were right there, in our house.

"Oh nonsense," my mother would say. She was Chinese and so she knew Communists—indeed some had been her friends long ago, she'd say. She said my American uncle had no idea what *real* Communists are like—this was one of her mysterious statements, impenetrable to this day. She knew Big Time, and it was not in the Hampton house. We had nothing to fear from my uncle. He and his wife lived a not-bad life and eventually retired to Palm Beach.

Right on the coastline road in Rye, stood Herb Philbrick's store. Formerly just a general store, it had been there since the dawn of the automobile and had been frequented by my great-grandparents in their day, in excursions from their house on Exeter Road. In 1952, Philbrick published the notorious book, *I Led 3 Lives* (i.e., *Lives* as a Communist, an FBI counter-agent, and a plain old businessman). This became a television series of the same name—at the height of the McCarthy-era hysteria about Communists. And though my grandparents remained staunch Republicans, they avoided the Philbrick store because Philbrick the spy and counter-spy had testified against Communist party members including my uncle, their own son (the son who ran for Congress as a Communist). Philbrick's store, with its conspicuous *I-Led-3-Lives* sign at the front, was a flaming reminder of all the fissures in my family. My grandfather would drive grimly past that store every time, disregarding backseat childish pleas to stop for ice cream. *No ice cream!* he'd bark.

Years later my sister married a member of the Progressive Labor Party which had split off from the Communist Party. Her husband and others in the Party had distributed leaflets to G.E. workers outside the plant in Lynn. My father wasn't happy about this, but after all: hadn't he himself married a Chinese girl, a decision equally appalling to his conservative parents? In time, my sister's husband trended rightward and became a Republican. Full circle.

6. Unspoken

On the station platform I see my old friend waiting for me, hands in his pockets, smiling. He's a bit thin now, a bit grizzled, but the incandescent smile hasn't dimmed much. He wants to talk, over coffee, but we can't talk long because he needs to get to his appointment at the hospital for chemo. The mercilessly revealing sunlight beating through the café window strikes us still harder when we go outside into biting wind and honking cars and people walking ducked against gusts of blowing grit.

As I walk away I'm taken back to another station, where over 50 years ago, the year the military draft swallowed its largest number of young men, I see my friend. It's spring. He's a young man, big smile, clean shaven, blonde hair trim, waiting on the platform eager to see me to hear about my job hunt in New York City. I'd stayed at the Waldorf in the bargain-priced quarters formerly for maids where bathrooms were shared and where at breakfast in the fancy dining room I was so rocked by the cost of a glass of orange juice (50 cents), poured for me by a waiter with a pitcher who hadn't even asked whether I wanted orange juice, that forever after I resist any hovering waiters threatening o.j. by pitcher.

That bygone Waldorf was in that bygone New York City, and there I walk bravely into the Pan Am hiring offices seeking a listed "management intern" job but I'm informed by a recruiter that they don't hire girls (his word). But behold I'm told I'm attractive enough and just barely tall enough to be a stewardess, and yet when I'm escorted into the claustrophobic reception area for stewardess applicants there is something depressing about the spectral flower arrangement on the reception desk, and the form I have to fill out feels ominous in its detail, so that after maybe fifteen minutes I simply stand up, straighten out my stockings as well as the nubby wool suit I'd purchased with precious dollars rationalized by no more than hope for the management intern interview, and then walk out of the stewardess office, walk back out of the building and onto Park Avenue still clutching the half-completed stewardess application form, back to Grand Central Station, where I catch the train for the five hours back to Boston. Where he greets me, at the station.

I make the job hunt funny in the telling, but it wasn't. To this day I think he never saw the disappointment in it. *What did I expect? A girl in management?* he may have thought, but I'm not being fair because that's the way we all thought back then, and I never thought to object. After all, for women the received wisdom of that time was to get married and probably pretty soon, so it didn't matter. Not back then. At least Pan Am didn't ask about color or race, the way a suitor might.

I end up going to grad school instead of working, because the fellowship I win pays more than any job I'm offered, though back then I wouldn't admit it to anyone.

And back then, not long after my New York City foray, my friend went into the Marines because the draft, deadliest in that year, had to feed the combat in Vietnam and he took the bull by the horns, he'd say. And once it was over he was lucky, he'd also say, because he lost only hearing, and only in his right ear. Next to where he'd held the rifle.

Beyond that he wouldn't say much, not about the war.

7. The Spread of Quicksand

I marry a Canadian, safely remote from the *sturm und drang* of War and Anti-War. Thus our wedding lacks political fireworks. But this is the year when Martin Luther King and Bobby Kennedy are assassinated, and student demonstrations are rife, and we are graduate students at Harvard, where faculty are being called to Washington by Congressional committees addressing the war in Vietnam. While my husband pursues economic theory, I study Communist documents issued in China. I read them in Chinese. These are filled with standard phraseology such as: *Running Dogs of Imperialism; All Reactionaries Are Paper Tigers; Grasp Revolution, Increase Production;* and the like—excellent background for my later sifting through audit-speak footnotes in financial statements, but again: that's another story.

In a graduate seminar I present a paper I've researched, which is criticized by all present, excepting one guy in the back who waits till the others leave to say to me, *Your paper is more right than they know.* It turns out he's there on leave from the CIA. Little do I know, at that moment, that the internal upheaval gaining steam in China, wherein the Chinese attack one another, is soon to be recognized as the Cultural Revolution. It poses negligible threat to the United States. But try telling that to those in the State Department and Defense Department who subscribe to the Domino Theory and prosecute the war in Vietnam.

Just three years earlier, an older friend is about to depart for Vietnam to join a so-called pacification program, the very phrase a theft of the word for peace because it was always about war. That summer there is a big victory for U.S. forces, body count 700 Viet Cong, they say—but the numbers make me wonder, and where did they ever get that *body count* idea, I ask, but my friend doesn't know or doesn't say. I see worry in his gaze. How do you do hearts and minds on the ground with bombs from the air and napalm, I ask, and he dodges. We go to a picnic on the banks of the Potomac River with South Vietnamese colleagues of his, and their families, and amidst the small children horsing around and demure wives unpacking lunch, I see that the Vietnamese man who introduces himself as The General is taut as a wire stretched to snapping point.

U.S. troop levels in Vietnam climb past 200,000, and draft boards across the country are grabbing anyone they can, young men who can't wriggle out with real or unreal medical exemptions or who can't hide in graduate schools. It's all that guys talk about these days, guys in college, guys facing mortal engagement that defies any dreams they once had.

I'm starting to grasp the stuff that my friend and his colleagues and friends discuss, always to the side, obliquely, covertly, and CIA crosses my mind more than once. I begin to get all the acronyms: ARVN, MACV, NLF, NVA, CORDS, USAID, DIA, DRV, GVN, I Corps, DMZ, all of these real, not gibberish. What was background noise in college now begins to take shape like some phantom from that jungle far across the sea where men are mired and suffering, whether in fatigues or in what they're calling black pajamas and I know that's a put-down and a whistle in the dark when the dark holds terror. Borders move by night, by stealth. Men fight and re-fight for the same ground. People are writhing, ARVN and NVA and Americans and always the Viet Cong, the indomitable VC. And civilians. Children shot, killed, collateral damage is the term, and my skin crawls when I look—at the photos, the evening news. The more I see, the less I know.

My friend left for that war, and he died.

IN MANY WAYS THE SUMMER DAYS ALONG THE NEW HAMP-shire seacoast were never far from war. Slightly northeast of Exeter, the Portsmouth Naval Shipyard built ten nuclear submarines, including the *Thresher* which was lost at sea with 129 aboard and mourned to this day. By that time, I was old enough to understand the scale of loss, so concentrated in our area. And Pease: mighty Pease Air Force Base, all muscle, which sent B-47 and B-52 bombers above our heads to defend us, as part of the Strategic Air Command network that flourished during the Cold War and the Vietnam War. Thus along the tiny seacoast of New Hampshire sat two of the three nuclear capabilities of that time. The only thing missing was the intercontinental ballistic missile. We grew up with Mutually Assured Destruction, nuclear destruction, the concept taught in classrooms, the acronym MAD the object of mirthless laughter. *Live Free or Die,* introduced to New Hampshire license plates in 1971, had special meaning.

Did all the nuclear weaponry, some of it locally pro-duced and all of it locally maintained, trigger-ready—did that weaponry buy us safety? Was there any way to escape the Cold War, this thing that took us to Vietnam? The War in Vietnam sundered my family. Maybe I should leave it at that—but wait:

My husband and young son and I were having lunch on the terrace of Saunders, the lobster house next to Rye Harbor. From there we watched as a pickup truck with a trailer was backing slowly down the boat ramp to take on a boat waiting in the water. There was some kind of snafu, and the driver got out to tweak something on the trailer, shouting to his young son in the passenger seat,

"Keep an eye out!"

Somehow the parking brake didn't hold firmly, and the truck started sliding backwards—slowly, slowly, slowly, down the ramp.

"Get the brake kiddo, hit the fucking brake!!" in voice of high alarm. But the kid only sat there, wide-eyed, frozen. The truck was now about to slide into the water, its rear end beginning to submerge.

Full panic: *"GET THE FUCK OUT OF THE TRUCK! GET OUT NOW! OPEN THE FUCKING DOOR AND GET THE HELL OUT OF THERE!!"*

The kid slid out and the truck slipped under the water. It completely disappeared. A few bubbles surfaced. We sat there electrified, along with all the other onlookers.

Then someone broke the silence, *They'll call a tow truck and they'll pull that truck out okay, and they'll clean out all the salt and shit, and get it back on the road okay. But that truck won't never be the same, no way.*

At the Fall of Saigon in 1975, my parents got out and got back on the road okay, but they were never the same, no way.

8. Exeter: Things Gone and Not Gone

Up the Rye coast, there was an abandoned concrete watchtower, a relic of World War II, when German submarines glided offshore and there were fears of a landing by Germans on our eastern shore (and Japanese on our western shore). At night coastal residents were required to use blackout curtains or otherwise only candlelight, to avoid detection by enemies in the water offshore. So the watchtower dated from those times, a crumbling, weedy eyesore. Today it's been transformed into a dwelling of architectural interest. Who'd know its history?

South of Rye Harbor are the fish houses of North Hampton, just below Little Boar's Head, where my grandmother would go every other day to buy fish that was demonstrably fresh. She insisted on such fish. Today those houses, or those that are left, are scrubbed and neatly shingled as never before, having survived not just salt and surf and rising sea, but also some heavy controversy about their very existence. The coastline today is threatened in a way we'd never imagined could happen—except by rising water of childhood nightmare.

Thus I look around while driving, seeing through memory's blurred lens the things transformed since my childhood here, and the things disappeared or lost to memory. The Coast Guard station on North Hampton beach? I need to check whether it's still there. What about the little beach cottage? Now surrounded by enormous neighboring houses. The mosquito-ridden woods across from my grandmother's Hampton house? Now a condo development. Applecrest Farm? Still there, check. The ice cream stand in Greenland? Gone. The Chinese laundry on Water Street that my mother wanted to go to but my grandmother did not? Gone. The colonial houses on High Street and the *grande dame* ones along Hampton Road in Exeter? They're still there, but they struggle or fail to stay single-family residences. My grandmother's bank, on Water Street, has changed its name, becoming part of a brand that goes far beyond Exeter, beyond New Hampshire. Across from that bank and downstreet a bit, the building that once housed Woolworth's five and dime store is still there, but not the store itself, where even in my childhood nothing could be had for only five cents or ten.

9. What I Learned From My Folks

Now I'm supposed to be old, but I'm not, and I have no idea how I got this far in life. My parents were cut down way earlier in their lives. So this is borrowed time, I figure. I want to use it well, try to do right by them. They tried hard, but failed in some ways to help my sister and me adjust to what we faced as not-white, not-Chinese.

But could I have done any better, given the world they lived in, the terrible things that happened to them, losing China which was my mother's life, and my father's too, even though he came from New England. You can spend your whole life trying to fix something that went wrong when you were young (even if it isn't your fault), and end up making it worse. I can say now, *Why didn't you just walk away from it, from your dreams of China the dreams that were destroyed?* But I don't know what it's like to lose my home country and everyone I knew, my whole family, my life as I knew it. And to be unable to go back until I was practically gone, a life lived with a searing absence like a hologram of imprisoned memories and an unquiet spirit exorcised only by writings. Writings kept hidden until almost the end.

That's my mother. In the evening she often listened to the Rachmaninoff Piano Concerto No. 2. No wonder.

Yet she could laugh, wring joy out of sodden flotsam and jetsam. She never complained, not to us, her kids. She never cried, except maybe once when we kids started bickering instead of helping her lug wood for the fireplace. *This doesn't happen in China,* likely she was thinking. *Where's the filial piety, where's the respect for parents?*

Breakdown.

And once more, later, when surgery removed her ability to have more children, and she reached for us from her hospital bed in Washington shakily repeating, *You're all I have. You're all I have.* My godfather told me years later that she was sure she'd die in that surgery, in that hospital, all alone in America. *Foreign* America, foreign to the end.

But otherwise in my lookback she was strong and resolute, brooking little frailty. In our nomadic way of life she was trying to set an example, amid her troubles, my father's disappointments, and the whiplash changes we lived with always. The gist was they had to be strong, my parents.

You figure this out when you have kids yourself and you try to act strong and bite your tongue about what's happening around you, terrible stuff and danger. You figure it out when you end up doing the same drill, all that silence, all that stonewalling, all that dancing around the subject. Doing it for the kids' sake, to protect them.

And it worked, at least it did for me, this kid. The naïf who eventually learned to live with strange identity; learned ambiguity; learned loss. It became routine.

10. Scattershot

It's not such a big deal, I hear you say. Of course not. I look white, and in most situations whites have more privilege than non-whites. So where's the problem? After all, I get to forget about race.

But I also get to hear the anti-Asian jokes, the caricatures of Chinese, the things people say when they think there are no Chinese present. In professional situations no one guesses I'm Chinese. So I get to decide whether to tell them deftly, humorously, or bluntly, or just let it go. Over decades of work, has it happened 2,000 times, or far more times? I don't keep book.

Even the child I was knows that in certain kinds of company I have to find some way to head off slurs, some subtle way to get across that I'm half-Chinese, and there are thousands of ways to do that. All because I don't want to hear anti-Asian jokes or slurs.

Scattershot, these things. Disappointments linked to who I am, not to what I did. Covert wounds but minor. Too much of a muchness to dwell on them, but they happened and they stick:

A babysitter looks at me and says she'd never have guessed I was half-Chinese, but now that she knows it, she can see that my eyes are sort of *chinky*.

I'm a kid in an argument with another kid when he asks a parent who's right and she points to me. *Well,* says the kid, *Three Chinese cheers! Fooey! Fooey! Fooey!* He isn't buying it and shouts his sarcasm to all the other kids.

I'm a guest at a party where an Air Force guy holds forth, telling a group of us that in flight training a bad landing is called *a Chinese landing* or *One Wing Low.* Laughter all around.

At my first fulltime job, which was as a career counselor, a young woman comes in for advice. She has an Irish surname, long straight brown hair and freckles, and there's the barest hint of Asia around the cheekbones. Well into the conversation I summon up a nervy question for her: would she by any chance be part Asian? And I tell her why I'm asking. The answer is yes, her mother is Korean, and in that flash of recognition we discover for a moment a someone in almost exactly the same position, a someone almost seamlessly white but not close to being white.

At my second job, the head of the organization comes into my office, closes the door behind him and nervously asks me would I mind too much if they put me down as Chinese for the affirmative action form they have to file. I say of course I don't mind. But he's clearly embarrassed for me and he apologizes.

During a charades game in the 1960s someone acts out the word *gook*, using his hands to slant his eyelids upward at their outer edges and miming the Viet Cong in pajamas, and the room hoots and hollers and I shut down.

At an investment meeting, someone says *It was a real Chinese fire drill*, describing the incompetent handling of a failed fund. People nod in agreement.

At another investment meeting, someone says *Never trust a Chinese, and don't try meeting with them because you can't tell who's who—they all look alike.* Laughter all around the table.

At the opera, the end of Madame Butterfly brings slow tears to my eyes as the American naval officer leaves his Japanese lover for his white American fiancée, and afterwards my companion says to me kindly, *I didn't know you identified so much with an Asian woman.* He means well, and I smile, but he's way wide of the message. So often I simply say nothing. Because it's too complicated to explain.

At a dinner party an elegant English woman speaks with exaggerated upperclass authority to inform the dinner guests that Chinese women detest hairy men, they don't think it's sexy, which means they don't favor white men. My white husband across the table suppresses a laugh.

At a Christmas performance of *The Nutcracker,* dancers playing Chinese men are wearing coolie hats and single pigtails down their backs, and they bob their heads and grin stupidly as they prance around like clowns. Afterwards I tell my children that Chinese men used to wear a pigtail because that was required by the Manchus who ruled China for over 200 years, sort of like having to wear a Star of David if you were Jewish, and when the Qing Dynasty finally fell, Chinese men all over the world cut off their pigtails right away. But my kids hadn't even noticed the pigtails. And because it's Christmas, I decide not to say more about the harsh caricature we'd just witnessed.

I've visited communities that are virtually all-white. The workers come from elsewhere. Often these places are vacation spots where people have second homes. At such a resort, I'm walking through a restaurant foyer with a Chinese friend, both of us dressed casually. A man, another diner, comes up to my friend and says loudly, *I need to speak with your supervisor.* At her startled look he realizes he's made a mistake and hurries off without another word. My friend brushes off the encounter as you'd brush off an insect. Our eyes meet as we return to conversation, walking away from embarrassment.

I take a DNA test to see whether a rogue European interloper might have gotten into the Chinese family tree, as an explanation for my failure to look Chinese. The test shows that I'm within 1% of being exactly half European, exactly half Asian. Half Asian means the interloper theory goes down the drain.

Sometimes it's funny. At a spa, a Chinese stylist plucks my eyebrows and says, *You know what, you have one Asian eyebrow and one western eyebrow, very hard to make same shape,* and I laugh and tell her I'm half Chinese. She looks startled, astonished.

One day I discover that a longtime friend's family wealth derives generations ago from a business that used Chinese laborers brought to California for menial and dangerous work no Americans would do for the pittance paid. The government denied citizenship to Chinese laborers, denied family, and the men most likely perished from exposure to poisoning inherent in their labor, worked to death in the full meaning of that phrase. At the moment of discovery, I keep my mouth shut although my spirit is shot through. Is my friend responsible for what his great-grandfather did?

You say *VC* and my mind goes to Viet Cong, but today it's just an asset class, venture capital. You say *dink* and my mind freezes around the slur reference to Viet Cong, but today it's just an acronym for Dual-Income-No-Kids, a market segment with lots of purchasing power. And so the war in Vietnam is pulled under by the forward motion of history, of heavy machinery plowing onward, pulling under what's past, burying it. Our language is subject to amnesia, and it's careless. But we who were touched by that war, whether directly or indirectly and however deeply, find it never far from our field of vision, our range of hearing, the terrain of where we learned loss and learned it too well.

NOW I WRITE AT DUSK, PONDERING SCATTERSHOT AND the cross-weave of identity and history, mixed with the toxic remains of the wars that tore at my family.

China and Later

Nine-Tailed Fox

*Maybe I was six when my father took me to the movie
I never forgot, the one with a magic monkey with a
terrible grin and whooshing a long metal stick. Then at
night a frail fishing boat pushes out into the inky lake,
only to be yanked down under the water's surface by
a giant hand that's risen upward out of the lake, and
then on the shore comes the fox with nine tails and all
the children in the theater shriek in terror and some
run out. I don't shriek. I sit still as stone, take it all in.
Later my mother said, Oh Joe, why did you take her
to that movie, and my father laughed and said It's just
an old Japanese movie. An old movie.*

G oing back to the beginning, I see my parents tossing
me into the back seat of their beat-up Army jeep,
then driving into the Chinese countryside beyond
the massive city walls of Nanjing, jouncing over dirt roads
surrounded by rice paddies and then up narrow byways to
obscure temples, many and yon. My father is young and
laughing. He lifts me off the jeep, and I climb the uneven
stone steps to the temple, hearing soft tones from the bells

ahead—keep on climbing—looking up at wheeling birds, smelling sweet incense when we reach the temple. And there at the end of our climb, standing or crouching—are the monsters, always the monsters. They're garish, baring sharp teeth, staring with bulging eyeballs and in contorted positions. One brandishes a broadsword at me. Some curl themselves around a tall column or hiss from above a gate I have to walk through. There's one with a lion's head on top of a horse's body but covered with snaky scales; *qilin,* my mother says—a chimera. I don't know it's not real.

Now I clamber over a high wooden doorstep and find myself in a vast temple where I see row upon row upon row of Buddhas and monsters and scholars, sitting or standing malignly or benignly, it doesn't matter—they all loom huge, and I am tiny. They tower above me as I walk solemnly down the rows, monsters glaring down at me, both sides. Even the mild carved-ivory scholar—my mother points him out to me, hoping to reassure—only frightens. That's because he isn't really a person, he's maybe a deer or a goat, only he's standing on his hind legs and wearing a scholar's robe. That gown doesn't fool me. This thing is as bendingly strange as all the others. He's making nice, but he is threatening, just like the others, only worse because he's pretending to be normal.

At home there are monsters too, smaller ones—statuary with grinning or grimacing faces, depending on how you look at them—guardian lions, my mother says. Guarding against evil spirits. A lion on each side of the door, lips drawn back over long teeth and curled tongue, and my mother points out that the daddy lion has a ball under his front paw, the mommy lion a cub under her front paw. They hulk right outside the door, to ward off the evil spirits.

My mother tries to wave away all the monsters I ask about, but my *amah,* Xiuying, always tells me stories and that's how I hear about the fox spirits, the shape-shifters, sometimes with nine tails and you can't tell the good foxes from the bad, she says. Just run away from them, she says.

My father laughs, liking to scare me and then telling me he's joking, don't look so worried. If I ask him a question, he needles, tells me anything's possible, any strange story, always with a laugh. He says he's teasing, but who knows, I'm a pretty serious kid, absorbing each new monster glowering in a dark temple or standing in a rice paddy with paws under water or looming as pillaged decoration in somebody's living room.

Outside our Nanjing home there's a war going on, and the People's Liberation Army has taken over the city on their road to victory. Food has been scarce for a long time. In the streets small children wear rags, and run untended, and beg for food. The Nationalist army has fled the city, but now they're using planes to bomb targets in the city they abandoned. Air raids send my mother rushing by pedicab to the day care center where I'm the only western kid, actually half-Chinese, *hun xue er,* speaking only Chinese like everyone else. My mother clutches me as our pedicab swiftly rattles home. I peer out at scrambling confusion in the streets, hearing loud siren blasts as shopkeepers and beggars alike run for cover, terror no less crazed for its dailiness. Once, one of these planes crashes at night, and next day my father takes me to look at the wreckage lying still smoldering in the street. A burned-out hulk of steel. A dead monster. My father takes pictures, just as he always does with monsters. About the bombing, my mother just says *mei shi, mei shi*—it's nothing.

Bombs falling from the sky, and later in Taiwan come earthquakes and typhoons, but at home my father distracts us by telling of other grim possibilities, landslides and volcanoes and disasters of all sorts. We're sitting at dinner under a lamp suspended from the ceiling, and when an earthquake rumbles he points to the lamp and we watch how far it swings back and forth, and he makes light of it while laughing. Earthquakes at night push objects off shelves to the floor, and once the wall to a room caved in. That's just Taiwan, my father says.

Over the years he adds stories from Edgar Allan Poe and Rudyard Kipling, giant bugs and lagoon creatures. Dire situations. Arthur Gordon Pym. Earthquakes that swallow men and horses! Soldier ants that turn sleeping people into skeletons! Strangers clomping up the back stairs! I sit there, taking it all in. Quiet. Furrow the brow. Hide any confusion. Then later on, hide knowingness too. Nobody's fool, but keeping mum.

A cool customer, my godfather described me when I was only three years old (this note I found in his papers, after his death at 100), still in China. He'd seen me laughing delightedly at his atonal attempts at Chinese pronunciation, at his challenges to me to correct him, which evidently I did with giddy authority.

But he'd also seen me looking askance, wary about the things that approached along the twisted road of my childhood. After all, the nine-tailed fox is a shape-shifter. *You never know.* Get used to it.

11. Last Boat Out of China

We leave China in a hurry. From our Nanjing home with its formal rooms we race by frantic pedicab to the station, take a train to Shanghai—my mother, little sister, and me. The station is desperately crowded with people trying to escape what's now obvious: the impending Communist victory over all China. People are shouting, people are shoving, men in uniform trying to push back, messy swamp of noise and confusion, a dog escaping its leash and getting lost in the crowds, owner running after it venting anguish. My eyes are almost level with lots of knees, knees belonging to people jostling all around me. And there's lots of stuff they're carrying: bulging suitcases, a tennis racket, a fur coat, a stiff little button-eyed teddy bear with a jagged space where an ear has been torn off. All kinds of stuff lugged by westerners and by some Chinese who are on the losing side of the civil war.

The poor who can't pay for tickets huddle atop the train, legs dangling from the roof, the things they hold dear wrapped in cloth. *Mei shi, mei shi,* my mother always says: it's nothing. It'll be all right, she says.

On reaching Shanghai, my mother carries two suitcases and my little sister and I walk in front of her, holding hands as we trudge up a gangplank and onto a crowded steamer sailing away from China, late September 1949, exactly "the last boat out of China" before the declaration of the new government. That boat is the *SS General Gordon,* an army troop ship that saw service in World War II and has hauled previous waves of refugees from Shanghai, before this last wave.

Inside, bunkbeds seem to climb up to the sky—troops' quarters now peopled by refugees thronging amid the babble of foreign words including English, which is still a foreign language to me. There's also a lot of Yiddish, I learn later, because most of the passengers are from the Jewish quarter in Shanghai, having already fled pogroms in Russia or genocide in Germany, and now the civil war in China. My mother and sister and I are assigned to quarters designated for women, where everyone waits for the bathroom, and yawning suitcases litter the floor. The air is fetid. I poke around the bunkbeds and see jewelry tucked away in the crevices, hidden there by some well-dressed women who'd grabbed the ornaments off their dressing tables in Shanghai. Now they're squirreling away their small stuff when their big stuff has been blown apart. Everything is tumultuous. Nothing is explained.

———

I'M FOUR YEARS OLD, A MERE SPECK IN A VERY LARGE world drama, a drama it will take decades for me to understand. I do not know, cannot know, that what I've just seen is the cataclysmic rupture of all things between the China of my mother, and the America of my father—a tectonic collapse that devastates my small family for the rest of my parents' lives.

12. After the Apocalypse

"Yea, though I walk through the valley of the shadow of death, I will fear no evil, for Thou art with me." During two years at a Church of Scotland school in Jaffa, the Arab quarter of Tel Aviv, we children loudly recite prayers and psalms while standing at attention every day during morning assembly and Bible readings, under the stern stare of Headmistress Miss Rosie. The kids are Israeli and Western, thrown together, no one but I seeing that the Valley of the Shadow of Death—still alive as I utter those words—is the valley between long rows of monsters on either side of me, as I'd walked beneath them, in a temple outside Nanjing, in another world.

In this world, Israel, the worry is about land mines. In that world, China, the worry was about bombs from the sky. In Taiwan, where we lived in the early 1950s just before Israel, the worry had been about the thousands of troops entering Korea from a place then called Red China while the US Army built a major garrison in Taiwan and flooded the island with its own troops, soldiers with guns everywhere, muddy roads, new barracks, new runways for new planes. This was the Korean War.

After China, we'd left Asia briefly and then we returned, to another war zone: Taiwan.

The airplane is big. It has four motors with blades going around so fast that they're just a blur and they whine so high-pitched your ears hurt. My mother says it's going to be a very long time in the plane. When it gets dark you can see an orange glow on the side of the four motors which I think is fire but my mother says don't worry, it's supposed to look like that. Later that night when everyone is asleep on the plane I hear big clanks and booms but I know my mother would just say it's supposed to sound like that, so I don't say anything especially because everyone is sleeping but me. But when the plane lands we aren't in Hawaii, we're in a place called Wake Island and one of the motors on the plane has turned black and it isn't going around anymore because it's dead. It caught on fire after all. My father says we're lucky to be on Wake Island because it's where military planes are refueled and repaired.

Active war zone, nearby war, and flight from war are stamped all over childhood. My small family soldiers on, as my father likes to put it. *Renao,* so exciting, my mother says, putting a positive spin on whatever situation comes along. I'd been eight when we left Taiwan, and by then, thanks to the US Army school in Taipei, I was as fluent in English as Chinese.

So to Israel. There are Palestinian refugee camps, on the radio the sinuous wail of Arab music, and hard black bread every day except Friday's sweet challah, all new to me. There's gunfire across the Sea of Galilee and unexploded land mines in Beersheba—*xiao xin!* be careful! my mother says. Near the Dead Sea, we pause at a lumpy column of mostly sandstone: Lot's Wife, another refugee (so my father says), frozen forever as a pillar of salt, looking blankly at the horizon.

We drive on to the Old City, Jerusalem, and cross the border at the Mandelbaum Gate where we weave our way around tank traps called dragons' teeth (more monsters) and towering coils of barbed wire everywhere, soldiers from both sides hauling machine guns and asking to see our papers, my father smiling cooperatively and then later telling us those guns could kill 100 people in as many seconds (thank you, Dad).

At King Solomon's stables on the Temple Mount in Jerusalem there are very few tourists. We've climbed a high wall, and I look toward the horizon in one direction, a long and rugged stretch to nowhere. Then I start running toward that nowhere. I start running away from family, along the high, stony rim atop the stables. My legs pumping and pumping, over jutting stones, I don't know where I'm headed, nor why I keep running on that high wall, aware that if I stumble and fall, the fall will be far down. *Unaware* that I could be mistakenly shot by one of the jittery soldiers. I hear the panic in the voices of my parents calling me back—"Ann! ANN! *AAAA-AAAN!*"—and still I run away from them. It is my first memory of scaring myself with my own decisions. Maybe it's the first sign of risk-taking akin to my father's. Daring the nine-tailed fox, learning to live with it. Always unsettled.

MONTHS LATER WHEN MY PARENTS DECIDE TO DRIVE TO Syria and Lebanon for several weeks, they drop off my sister and me at a kibbutz where we join children living in dormitories away from their parents, and working in the fields when not in class. Some parents at the kibbutz are Sabras, but most are refugees from the Holocaust. At the long tables at mealtimes, there are not enough table knives to go around. I wait until the person next to me has used the knife and then passes it along to me. I wait for the salt passed hand to hand, because there is no butter to put on the bread. The grownups are talky, full of the future, an irrepressible spirit expanding the room.

Dad wants to find coins, old Roman coins he says. So when we go swimming at Herzliya and Ashkelon and even Acre, on the beaches we always keep an eye out for old coins. Sometimes we look around Roman pillars fallen into the sea, waves washing over the history of it all, which Dad explains to mostly deaf ears—we just want to go swimming. At Acre we're climbing around the ruins and he tells us about the famous prison, how not long ago the British were not allowing Jewish refugees to come here, and some Jewish fighters blew up the prison, and we don't get any of it. We can't follow it, we're impatient, don't tell us about all this *stuff* just let us play.

In the Ramat Gan neighborhood of Tel Aviv, we play with kids who live nearby, Daniel and Deborah whose family has immigrated from Montreal to Israel. And Joshua, whose parents fled Germany. There's Lambros, from Cyprus, who does household chores; and an occasional housemaid named Bella, from Rumania, who sings and flirts with Lambros as she does the ironing. My best friend at school is from Bulgaria, another from Poland, yet another from Czechoslovakia.

We who play do not yet know our families' stories, and these kids, my friends, are children born of survivors amidst the ashes of families lost, left behind, killed. There are stories within stories, but children are too young to be told horror, and the parents cannot speak of it, not yet. Let children be children and pray for their future.

So we run up and down the hilly street, around looped corners sometimes giving onto vacant lots that look cratered, and then in and out of our backyards. At the top of the street is the Soviet Embassy, a glum concrete building with heavily draped windows and surrounded by a high fence with barbed wire on top. There are large guard dogs. At night we hear Russian movies boomed from the flat rooftop where embassy employees and their families sit to watch movies from their homeland. Sometimes late at night, from our homes we hear the howling of guard dogs, which makes us uneasy. We are in a time of strange things. When once huge swarms of locusts rain down hard from the sky, we all run for our Bibles and ask what we've done wrong, half-joking and not.

In the bombed-out, lushly overgrown hillside next to our house we play hide-and-go-seek. We also play army, with Danny always the general who commands our forces. Who are we fighting? "Enemies"—just nameless enemies. The low-bending limbs and enormous leaves of castor trees reach over our troop movements, giving us jungle cover as we scramble over fallen masonry and clutching roots. We're told the beans, bunched as swollen nettles on the tree limbs all around us, would make excellent castor oil. We grimace because we've heard castor oil is nasty.

Later we're told to stop playing in that overgrown lot, because one of the parents has worried aloud about unexploded mines. And my mother has an ear for danger, always.

So instead we play Pitcairn's Island, just my sister and I, using a garden hose to inundate the small garden, the island, beside the front walkway to our house. Softened by water, the earth can be reshaped into mountains and roads and rivers where the garden hose supplies endless water. We use garden plants for jungle. We use small sticks to represent the people on the island, people who as in that novel are mostly white men and brown women, come to think of it now. They live hard and fight hard and have one crisis after another. It is enthralling. We play wild, stoked by imagination, making up stories, sometimes using our own vocabulary, for hours totally focused on a combative world of our own making.

A few years later, at Christmas, Dad gives us a board game called *Risk*. It does not play wild. It involves military strategy and armies doggedly seeking to dominate the world. In the version of the game we have, the armies can get very big and cumbersome, the game turning into near-gridlock, any action slow and ponderous.

Some games of *Risk* are abandoned. Kids are bored, want faster outcomes. Adults stay with it, trapped.

13. Riptide: Washington

Then in 1956, my family is told to pack up and evacuate from Israel. It's just before British and French forces, along with the Israeli army, attack Egypt. It's the Suez crisis, the Sinai War. We leave our house and stay with friends while waiting for the plane that will fly us out of Tel Aviv. I'm told nothing because I'm just a kid, but I know the urgency of it because of the talk between my parents: we need to go, go back to America.

I'm now 10. At the friends' house in Tel Aviv where we await evacuation, I sit in the formal living room and carefully turn the pages of *Life* magazine to look at pictures of the country I've scarcely seen. Thus in that fraught time I learn Tales of America, such as the passenger ship *Andrea Doria* sinking offshore near the port of New York where it was headed; and an explosive device planted in a New York City subway train, leading to talk of a so-called Mad Bomber putting big round bowling balls (in my mind) under subway seats. So: America isn't safe either, it seems, and this is even before I learn that half-Chinese is called half-breed by bullying boys, once they see my mother in her Chinese *qipao,* the "Suzie Wong" dress. Soon enough I learn that I'll never be just like everyone else—which had been my hopeless dream. Race is the buried fault line across my entire childhood.

Now I can ask: did my parents keep us abroad to avoid the race discrimination in America? The civil rights movement meant nowhere to hide. Abroad in nonwhite countries we were hidden in plain sight, where brown faces and mixed blood and colorful dress and folklore and magic and mysterious cultures were thrown together so that no one was different, because everyone was different.

In Washington we are different. My family is different. I am different. Whenever my mother shows up at school, in my classroom, the kids' heads swivel in my direction with startled expressions because my mother in her *qipao* doesn't look like anything they've seen before, in these all-white schools. They think she's wearing a costume.

In a documentary film shown in sixth grade, I watch a black and white newsreel of teeming crowds of starving Chinese, and I think for the first time: *those are my people! Those people.* Big discovery: they are in terrible shape, those people, so unlike our neat and tidy classroom with neat and tidy kids. Those not-white people in the movie are suffering, and this is because they are Communists, says the voice-over. Suddenly I don't belong in that neat and tidy classroom. But with my brown hair and freckles, no one knows unless I tell them or unless they see my mother.

My mother: proud, pragmatic, stubborn. Proud of her heritage, her widely admired family in China. Pragmatic about an adult life far less prestigious than her childhood. Stubborn about prevailing, come what may. No showing weakness. No time for regret. Too much to live for, a life full of surprises and curveballs. Distantly loving with her children. Joyful and laughing with friends. Quiet when there was nothing good to say.

Now suddenly my mother doesn't want to talk much about China. She's afraid because in America it's the Cold War, no more hot war. My father works in the State Department, that formidable building with long polished corridors that I've visited only once. The Cold War means you can lose your job if people think you're a Communist, and on TV and in the newspapers they're saying the Chinese are Communists. Yet at home I hear not *all* Chinese are Communists, but it's all so complicated—my mother says—that it's best to talk only about my American relatives, not that I even know my Chinese relatives. My Chinese relatives are not for discussion. I don't know what to think. I don't know what to say. So I don't say much.

All I know is that being half-Chinese is something I have to be careful about. Cold War. Civil Rights. Race. These things make my parents choose their words carefully, I can tell. My mother is sure of herself as always, but she is now telling us we need to be careful what we say, so that people don't get the wrong impression. I keep learning to say little, learning to say nothing.

When Civil Rights marches begin to spread, and talk of civil rights for black citizens begins to dominate the conversation at home (my mother and father both strongly in favor), tensions rise in the Washington area where our very modest bedroom community has no residents of any color but white—excepting my mother, it seems. It doesn't matter, my mother says. But it does matter. She has no idea what it's like not to look like what you are. And now conversations are more and more about race. I grow even quieter, so quiet I'm barely there.

Before a family trip driving south through Virginia to Colonial Williamsburg, my parents sit us down and tell my sister and me to be careful, and not to worry if our family is asked to leave a restaurant or a motel. Not to worry if other people act angry when they look at us. My parents explain that some people don't understand a family with different-looking people, but just pretend it's okay, and do as they say. That's the drill. We're mystified. It turns out that while we turn heads, no one asks us to leave any restaurant or diner or store or hotel. Then in our family the whole subject, the whole problem, is submerged from view beneath the stuff and stuffing of our daily lives.

But we leave Washington. We leave the U.S., we leave The States, we're off to Nigeria. We're on the move again.

My parents were always on an adventure. They cherished their daughters and maybe also sometimes disregarded their daughters, in their unstoppable moves throughout our childhood. Or did they move to protect us from living in a country, in a Washington D.C. where so many wouldn't accept not-white, and where race popped up in everyday conversations? Or did they think they could leave behind the Cold War anti-communist investigations in Washington that threatened my mother's family and my father's career? Dinner table conversations at home were opaque and evasive when it came to questions about moving, questions about why we kept having to leave everything behind. We were kids, they said, and it was too complicated for us. Someday we'd understand, they said.

Now I understand this. *The civil war in China exiled my family. The Cold War kept us on the move. The Vietnam War, for my family, was the final riptide that drowned all hope of peace with Asia and reunion of far-flung family. It was not to be.*

In a world full of war and secrets and danger, where at each new childhood home I start out feeling like an outcast among strangers, fear can't get in the way of living: I have no choice, so I walk with it and run with it. The monsters of back-when, they speak to calculated risk, or sometimes not even calculated, just intuitive risk-taking, but conscious. I want to break away. Maybe that's what my father wanted us to do. After all, he'd broken away himself from his conservative Boston family, going to China during the Japanese invasion, learning Chinese, and then marrying a so-called Chinese girl from Beijing.

14. On My Own

It's 1961, I'm 15 and suddenly at a very odd boarding school north of New York City, for most of the year. My parents have sailed off to Nigeria, leaving me with my grandparents until classes start at the school. A year later we students hear that we're on the brink of nuclear war: the Cuban Missile Crisis. The headmaster tells us that because we're 90 miles from New York City, we're well beyond the danger zone. This gives us little comfort, and some parents come to pick up their kids just in case. If there was any doubt before, it's now clear that my family is gone, and gone to safer distance. My parents don't call me, because they're in Lagos, and because overseas calls are way too expensive and we never had much money.

Besides, what is there to say? Given the situation, the words *I love you*, completely absent in our household vocabulary, would only spark terror.

Come summer I go to Lagos, back to family although I've actually left them, left home, now keeping my own counsel. I listen politely and go my own way, sometimes without clue or caution, but never without both.

Lagos is fast-moving and my time there is short. I begin to date, and my friends and boyfriends are American, Nigerian, and Pakistani; English, Danish, and Egyptian. There's high-life music, dancing to tunes strangely upbeat for bearing loaded lyrics about Patrice Lumumba, jilted taxi drivers, jobs in the city, proto hip-hop maybe, who knows, there's a driving beat.

Royal Dutch Shell and Phillips Petroleum are sniffing around, but oil isn't in the picture yet. The long, narrow road from Lagos to Ibadan is through deep jungle and strewn with rusted-out hulks of wrecked cars by the wayside. The biggest danger is just the driving: avoiding the speeding trucks and ramshackle open-air buses taking farm women with their vegetables to market. Two-lane roads with such poor visibility that to pass the vehicle ahead is to risk death, never mind the merry wave of the driver ahead, beckoning you to pass him to your doom.

I'm young, my friends too, and we laugh about danger, in careless summertime, boundless sunshine only rarely interrupted by slashing torrential rains amid air of such palpable density it sends the family dog whimpering under the furniture.

My summer job is at the American Embassy, where I type memos and correspondence for a diplomat at his first posting. Occasionally he asks me to decipher my father's notoriously unreadable instructions, paper-clipped to a telegram. I'm chided by a Marine security guard for crumpling a low-level classified memo and tossing it into the wastebasket instead of using the burn bag.

Standing next to the teletype machine one August day in 1964, suddenly I hear it spring to action as the print-head chatters out the typed words *U-S-S-Maddox-attacked-by-North-Vietnamese-torpedo-boats-in-Gulf-of-Tonkin*. Each of those hammered words, slammed down like fists on a table, will drive the decisions and fates of many I knew and would come to know. That teletype message is the grim meteor in the distance, which later crashes into the backyard.

Not long after we leave Lagos, there's a military coup. A close friend's father, a Yoruba senator and Oba, is pursued by rebels into the expansive gardens of his estate, scattering the peacocks that wandered the lawn for show—but he is spared execution. Soon after comes the civil war between Nigeria and Biafra, during which a million Biafrans die of starvation or worse. By then my father has been reassigned to Washington, and is soon to become involved in the war in Vietnam, the Gulf of Tonkin Resolution having soon led to the arrival in Vietnam of American combat troops, boots on the ground, along with massive American bombing from the air, Rolling Thunder.

War. Everywhere we go is tinged, driven, or consumed by it.

Where to go with this? Interruptions, relocations, threats come out of nowhere, so make sure your expectations are all over the map, call them contingency plans, because actual plans shatter every time. No victory pumps, because the future arrives to whip you around, pull the rug out from under, but still you go onward, constantly recasting any target. The only certainty is yesterday. Competition? Besting others is a snare, because you wind up accepting zero-sum for no good reason.

And besides, winning can be deeply painful when the history is perverse. As when it became clear that I'd won the long argument with my father about the Vietnam War, this clarity driving silent tears down my face in a business school classroom, no joy in victory—but that was years later, another story.

In my first year of college I see a movie *The Loneliness of the Long Distance Runner* wherein a top competitor decides—as he's about to reach the finish line—just to stop cold. To stop running for others' cheers. Not to race against others. Not to win. This speaks to me. Further, I don't measure success by money gained. Not surprising, because in my parents' world view, money is disdained. Competing in business to make money isn't worthy of discussion, much less encouragement. Money simply isn't interesting. It never even crops up in family conversation. It's not what to focus on. And so I live a fundamental quarrel with Western competitive culture, maybe sprung from traditional Chinese values, or maybe from my parents' maverick leanings, or maybe from something else.

STARTING COLLEGE, I'M 17. IN THE FRESHMAN PHOTO book my picture is casual, blurry, my straight hair partly across my face because I was turning away from the camera, this photo unlike all the other girls' formal high school senior photos. My home town reads *Lagos, Nigeria*, also unlike all the others. Soon a Sigma Nu sophomore from MIT phones to chat me up and fish for a date, but then he asks with an aw-shucks chuckle if I could possibly be African, and I say no, it's just that my dad's in the embassy there, but I'm half-Chinese. Silence. Discomfort. So I add *I'm not joking and hey—I gotta run.* Later I think: I need to work on this, need to be clever, need to be witty, need to be charming, and it's all too much, too much about race.

In my junior year I transfer to Princeton for Chinese language study unavailable at my own college. I arrive both naïve and not. Princeton in 1965 is all male. No women students other than we twelve who study Critical Languages. No women faculty. No women deans. No women counselors. My parents, thankful that I'm on scholarship, studiously ignore that Princeton is all male—they never even discuss that. Not a peep. They only discuss which Chinese courses I will take. And so I arrive at Princeton, a little red riding-hood carefully ignoring any possible wolves. If they're there, they're just like the monsters: to be expected, not to worry, my mother has always said—though she does not say it when she bids me goodbye at the gloomy Victorian house on Library Place where they put up the twelve women. Perhaps I catch a fleeting look of concern on her face as I enter yet another world completely foreign: this time, a men's college.

Why did I go to a place where there were only 12 women students, over 3,000 men? When did change, even risky change, begin to beckon? Why do I court unease?

During Senate hearings for a Supreme Court nominee who may or may not have made unwanted advances on a girl at a party when both were teenagers, I suddenly receive an email from a long-ago friend. I haven't heard from her in years. She wants to know if anything like this had happened to me while at Princeton back in 1965-66; she copies her query to a few other women. I answer no: nothing like that had ever happened to me at Princeton. There were hijinks, plenty of drinking by plenty of men, and boisterous parties, and sometimes asinine remarks about women, but minus alcohol most of the men were simply eager, friendly, or indifferent, and a few extraordinarily kind. So I'd never been physically pressured or attacked. And yet, instinctively I'd known there were monsters there—not the men but the *situations,* the situations with possible monstrous outcomes. But long ago I'd learned to live alongside very bad possibilities, taking care, judging risks, going my own way.

Impassive to disturbing remarks, unfamiliar situations, I make myself hard to read, especially when there's pressure. *"Inscrutable!"* a guy might laughingly say to me, once they learn I'm half-Chinese though I don't look it. Maybe looking white invites jokes about Chinese because they're confident I'll react white. *Ha! an inscrutable Oriental, hardy-har-har.* That time another guy chimed in softly, in an attempt at a compliment, *Actually you're a real contribution to the gene pool, a very smart mix.* Which sounds like a discussion of horse breeding. But by now I'm tough. Sometimes it seems I can sober someone up just by being real, when another might giggle, flirt. I'm no good at flirting, but I might make a joke about an actual danger, and the hook is it's real; and it's exotic.

This off-the-wall upbringing, in dangerous parts of the world—it's not all bad. I get used to being underestimated, just a minor character back behind those who seek limelight. I'm back behind the noise, behind the stage, always gauging the situation. Limelight's dangerous; savoring congratulations only invites ruin. Have I learned this from my father who never speaks of his work? Or from my mother who always salts high expectations with some foreboding that denies success until well in hand?

Later I realize my mother had come from a generation of Chinese who have an uneasy relationship with success, not wanting to attract evil spirits or to tempt fate (as they say in the West). Chinese who often understate success as they understate fear. Who don't recognize defeat. Who survive.

Thus by college I'm deeply wary. I can usually sniff out potentially bad situations, taking notice in order to avoid them: sketchy surroundings; pushy men; too much alcohol;

dark empty streets in unfamiliar cities; rackety rollercoasters where friends jump on and beckon. Yet some things bite you anyway—the abrupt collapse of a close relationship, business betrayals, fatal car accidents, sudden death from cancer discovered too late, the long and utterly heartbreaking decline of parents too young to be so very damaged by circumstance, bound in deep sorrow by the detritus of wars fought badly, reversals of fortune, China lost to them forever.

15. Family

In the small grove of my birth family, there were four trees, and when that first tree fell the others swayed with shock, took the blow, tried to hold up the fallen tree, tried not to see the severed exposed roots and the oncoming death nine years away. Moss grew. Birds flapped. We tried seeing through branches to sunshine but our grove couldn't sustain itself.

In the mid-80s my mother had a stroke that left her forever unable to speak a sentence or to walk. At 71 she'd been a whirlwind of energy, stories, laughter infused by her special mischief which was Chinese lore. When she was stricken, my youngest child was not yet two.

My mother's stroke exposed and hastened my father's decline. My children never knew my parents before they both were leaning over, roots up, and then gone. My children never heard their grandparents' stories.

Many stories, so many stories, not all of them told. Many were obscured, some by design. Stories tucked away in boxes or stored as malleable memories in our heads. Our little grove, our little band of family, kept moving on. Until it stopped dead.

Do groves travel? you ask. Silly question. Ours did. We put down roots wherever we lived, but the roots were shallow, easily uprooted. My mother fell, and then my father. The stories became frozen, some skeletal, some hoary with time. They became baggage. I'm putting mine down.

Just two trees left now, two sisters, from the family we once were. We were of mixed race. We'd moved almost every other year. When we were young, war nearly always swamped us or lurched close by or loomed at distance. Sometimes war drove our family moves—civil war in China, Korean War, Second Arab-Israeli War, Lumumba's assassination in the Congo, the war in Vietnam. And the Cold War.

I struggle to give some presence to the ephemeral remains of a family that was seldom present because it kept moving.

We existed. We were a family.

16. Ghost Travel

Do I ever go back to China? I'm often asked. Well, yes. I've gone there to meet my family—a large and complicated family—the family lost to me and barely discussed during my childhood, effectively hidden from us children. Most of my Chinese grandmother's family, the Liang family descendants excepting my mother, live in Beijing, where my mother was born. My first sight of them in Beijing was 48 years after that abrupt and fevered departure from Shanghai on the *U.S.S. General Gordon.* There have been visits since then, and now waning hope for future visits to Beijing. Our family may well be riven again.

In marrying into the Liang family, my grandfather Zhou (or Chou or Chow or Chew, take your pick of English spellings) officially became Chinese. He was an adventurer of sorts, a Chinese-born Malayan, the youngest of three brothers. His career took him from family business to political aide to diplomat to investor, in Penang, Beijing, Rangoon, Manila, Ottawa and elsewhere. He died at the hands of Japanese soldiers in occupied Beijing. There's a tomb to honor him in Beijing's Wan An Cemetery, the tomb itself once knocked over by Red Guards but now under restoration with a family genealogy, to be carved into granite, that includes our *English* names along with our Chinese names. A family reunited on a tombstone, after the deaths of two generations.

So of course there are ghosts. But they're in the stories, not by the graves. They live on in the writings, the letters, the photos and mementos that my mother chose to save.

There's a long-ago photo showing her stylishly dressed in silk *qipao* with short raw silk coat and looking yonder while her companion, a tall young man, strides confidently toward the camera. Who is this man? Who took the picture? And another showing a grinning American in a beret, driving a jeep, cigar between knuckles as he grips the steering wheel. Who is this man?

Should I keep these photos, as she did for the rest of her life? These are ghosts from Beijing when it was Peking. They traveled with her through all those moves through all those years. Yet maybe they were actually forgotten, left to molder among her papers while she moved ever forward. But ghosts they were, because she couldn't go back, and she wrote often about ghosts.

Even if I can't travel now to Beijing to see my Chinese grandmother's family, my grandfather's family is reachable if I were to travel to Malaysia or to England to see two cousins, both architects, part of a large Chew family diaspora. We're brought together by zoom calls among Kuala Lumpur, Cambridge U.K., Beijing, and Exeter.

Travel and zooms are not the only way I go back, however. Going back is now unpredictable, random, whenever I hear the sound of Mandarin, *Putonghua*, spoken on the streets of Chinatown or elsewhere, this sound striking something deeply hardwired even as I continue doing whatever I'm doing at the moment. If I'm with someone, I don't mention the shimmer of memory that paints over my present with distant past, a glaze on my vision. And I keep re-learning Chinese, because I never completely lost it, and because it's home—to me.

But home was both comfort and mystery, and ghosts. And when I pass the elderly Chinese man seated by a path in the Boston Public Garden playing the *erhu,* the traditional two-stringed Chinese instrument poised vertical on his leg, I turn around and walk right back to put money in his glass jar. It's because the *erhu's* music is eerie; it evokes ghost visitations of the past, Chinese streets of long ago, a very little girl sitting on a Ming Dynasty granite lion in a faraway field, looking worried as though she already knew the years of upheaval to follow.

17. Lacrimosa

Over and over, we'd start together in a new place we were supposed to call home, and we'd do all we could to make it Home.

That is gone.

We'd know no one at our new schools but always knew each other.

That is gone.

We played games with one another, with whatever was at hand—dolls, cards, sticks, tin cans, mud, marbles, cardboard, water, pots and pans, inedible candy. Our imaginations never failed to deliver hours of happy involvement.

That is gone, with childhood.

During parents' cocktail hour we'd sing a tune from the movie *White Christmas (...there were never more devoted sisters),* dancing also, sometimes singing and dancing for their friends.

That is gone.

Sometimes our voices would rise in quarrel, until parents had to intervene.

That is gone.

Because we kept moving from one fraught country to another, without parental help to stay connected to those we left behind, we lost nearly all our childhood friends.

They are gone.

We ran on the beach, one after another, stepped gingerly on a rope-and-plank footbridge over rushing water, holding hands.

That is gone.

As teenagers, in separate countries for reasons of schooling we wrote one another letters describing our doings. We eagerly anticipated the reply letters, the responses to one another's thoughts.

That is gone.

As young mothers, on Christmas Eves, after our children and husbands had gone to bed, we'd stay up, wrapping endless kids' presents into the small hours, laughing and talking with hush so as not to wake the kids.

That is gone.

Gathered in the kitchen, with our kids we'd share funny stories about the foibles of our parents, to our kids' uproarious delight.

That is gone.

Now only silence. Our childhood together has dwindled down to striking photos taken in China or Manila or Taiwan or Israel or Nigeria, of a Chinese woman and an American man, and their seemingly unalike daughters.

18. Vietnam: Requiem

In a glaring Boston supermarket in the late 1970s, my mother and I run into someone abandoned in Saigon when the helicopters lifted out the Americans from the roof of the Embassy, and the Vietnamese woman greets my mother at first with joy, then suddenly deep hurt, strong grip of betrayal. It is there: in her eyes. The pain in her eyes holds, and it holds long and longer until finally my mother is forced to look down and away.

Encounters with soul-drenching war guilt, the outcomes from lives lived in tumult and defeat and bad choices seen only in hindsight—these are the monsters, the real monsters one deals with in order to keep going.

What about my father, who lived a life of risks and who involved his children in many of those risks: was he simply trying to teach his daughters how to live with risk? Were the monsters and scare stories just some kind of wacko child-rearing technique? Ghosts were powerful presences in China when I was a child. Ghosts were feared; often they didn't mean well. The monsters in the temples or by the doorway were to guard against such evil spirits. But those evil spirits, were they not there because of some past wrong committed by someone in the household? Or simply punishment for hubris?

My father was kind despite his teasing. He was deeply knowledgeable, tormented by the fallout from his own decisions. A good man who dared his way down a blind alley. Was his enormous bet on the war in Vietnam a misguided ideological fight? Or was it a doomed attempt to rewrite his personal loss of China, by succeeding in Vietnam? Or was it just one more adventure to a man who'd always sought adventure, free now from the burden of young children, free to land in the Mekong Delta just a few months before the Tet Offensive. It was the year before my marriage at age 22 that my father placed that last big bet of his professional life. The one that forever destroyed whatever peace of mind he'd sought, whatever hopeless cause he'd silently pursued. When defeat was imminent, he worked hard to evacuate South Vietnamese families. And the record hints he did try to counter some of the worst of the military's decisions. He failed. Then he died from the after-effects of Agent Orange, first stricken at age 65.

Now this: throughout his life, my father had said almost nothing about his work. It had always been a mystery, and it remained so after his death. The truth, if it is the truth, eludes capture. It darts in and out of early recollections and even adult memories. It's a guess and a dark possibility. It bore the weight of the Cold War that ruled my parents' lives, and dwelled in the deep hostilities and risks on both sides of the Pacific: McCarthyism in the U.S., the triumphant rule of the Communist Party in China. At dinnertime, the conversation about family relocations had always veered away from the truth, that central momentum that drove our lives. Little was asked and whatever questions asked were ducked. Childhood was swamped by mystery and irony and the wars that dogged us without end. If the good guys can be bad guys, and the bad guys good, then there's no good or bad, just the smoke of memory and sleight of hand. *You never know.*

And this: the truth shows up in plain sight, a passerby on the street given no attention in the moment. A Vietnamese woman in the supermarket. A drenched raincoat on someone just come from the approaching storm. Background noise at a formal dinner at the British Ambassador's Residence in Saigon. The talk at dinner was of opening a Hilton Hotel in the city, while beyond the wine and chatter and laughter was the insistent thumping of artillery. Later, when I asked my father about the nearness of war, he said with a shrug, "Oh, that. That just goes on every night." As though it were nothing, as though it were ordinary to hear warfare at a formal dinner. As though his position at the American Embassy made uncertainties dead certain.

Sixteen months later came the Fall of Saigon, desperate helicopters reaching skyward from the American Embassy, bearing Americans including my father. They left an embassy hastily stripped of important papers, left empty offices with severed phone cords, paperweights and official tchotchkes thrown about, the walls suddenly plaintive with photos of men in suits and men in uniforms shaking hands with one another.

Thus my father was felled by the ghosts of his early decisions, the truths he kept hidden but that dwelt in the evil spirits of my childhood: war, endless war, the nine-tailed fox. Yet don't I have my own ghosts and evil spirits, created in the course of a life in which I've taken risks, misjudged monsters, sometimes created hurt despite intense efforts not to? Or is it just that from childhood the teachings of the Church of Scotland somehow got mixed up with Chinese folklore? My parents sought folklore, never encouraged religion, maybe saying religion is folklore and you can choose, after you grow up. Waving it all away.

So despite all the uprootings, the dangers both real and unreal, there's choice in not believing in shape-shifting ghosts yet seeking them.

Running atop that wall: *Go forward or fall off this earth.*

Epilogue

Lost Language

They tell me: when I was age one, my mother and I arrived in Nanking, eight years after the notorious massacre. Japan had laid waste the city, but was finally defeated. Then came China's civil war.

When I was three, my mother and baby sister and I were evacuated to a camp in Manila, only to return to Nanking months later.

When I was close to four, the People's Liberation Army took Nanking, soldiers camping next door to our house on Sikang Road.

I see soldiers walking in single file, not marching. Slumping. A few break away to strip off their uniforms, right on the street, then run away into the crowds. I see this. Afterwards other soldiers in different uniforms march by, walking tall. They carry farm implements, rifles, rice in burlap bags slung over their shoulders. Their shoes are cloth. Some people clap their hands, others stand silent. I see this and I'm told that.

But what I grasp is the fear, the sweat of it and the smell of it. Soldiers are all around. War is all around, civil war, and soon the People's Republic of China will be born. Some people shout and sound angry; other people sing and sound happy.

You remember this, urgent, and it sounds like an order. My *mama* and *baba* are always telling me things, telling me to stay safe, and of course it's in Chinese, so Beware is *xiao xin! jin fang*! and Nanking is *Nanjing.* Chinese was my language and it stays forever, but its words and music are buried alive, where memory rises from fear so deep it's instinct. Fear tamed but snarling; fierce animal bursting out of a wastebasket. I make it normal.

In Nanjing every day I'm at school, where there's a dirt yard, some swings, and lots of little kids. Whenever we hear that wailing up-and-down sound—first soft then louder *louder louder* like a looming monster, coming from all around, an all-devouring siren—everyone runs flailing and crying, into the wooden schoolhouse. Once inside, my fright makes me stare stone-still and silent at the grain of the plank floor, because I think if I'm still enough the bombs won't find me. Then Mama sweeps in like wind and pulls me up in her arms, back into the pedicab to rush home before any bombs fall on us. The driver pedals fast and looks back over his shoulder, terrified.

Now we hear the boom-booms but not nearby. Mama says don't worry, it's just the flying tigers, and so I see orange-striped tigers swooping by on big black wings. Mama says flying tigers don't want to drop bombs on little girls. But at home whenever we hear that up-and-down wail, Mama cries *feiji! feiji!* airplanes! airplanes! and we crouch under the nearest table. Always I hunker down still as a statue, staring at the floor, the wood grain warping from fear, distant booming and the roar of tigers overhead. When Mama tries to hug me close, I shrug myself away so that I can stay staring downward. To keep the bombs away.

Flying tigers that don't harm little girls, this doesn't make sense. A few years later when I ask Baba, he says they weren't flying tigers at all, just soldiers in airplanes who didn't like the soldiers camped next door to our home.

Home is a small formal house with a bare stone courtyard where the cook keeps a duck in a very large wooden tub filled with water. It's *my* duck, I think, and each day I drop to my knees beside the tub and splash the duck and laugh wildly to see it move away, maybe flapping its wings but always swimming back toward me. I don't bother with the chickens running around—too skittish, too screechy, too hard to reach. Sooner or later their heads always get chopped off by the cook. No one tells me the duck comes next.

One morning the water in the tub is still, the duck gone. First stooping, then on hands and knees I search every part of the stone courtyard, soon unable to see because the tears have come, and then comes the sobbing for everything changing, always changing, everything I don't understand. I can't stop the wailing.

I don't know about the slow scraping agony of death-hunger, people ravaged by war, but Mama hears me howling and comes. She doesn't hug now, just brisk and no nonsense, she sits on her heels before me and says softly at first, *An, An, meiguanxi,* it's okay, some people took the duck and ate it because they're too hungry, that's all.

When still I cry, her voice toughens: stop crying, *ku meiyong,* it's just a duck. You're lucky, she says, lucky to have food to eat, *ni dongbudong,* you understand? Lucky!

I choke back my cries, dim them down to nothing. Her arm around my shoulders now, together we watch as a skeletal rat skitters past, scratching dust. I don't flinch. No more crying. But the rat comes back later as a nightmare where tigers wail while people race rats for food. The duck I see through other eyes now, hungry.

In this way, where I come from is China, by way of war. For reasons of race and geopolitics and perhaps risky choices, my family was swept under by the Cold War, the demented offspring of anti-communism that led to Vietnam, where humanity and hope perished. Today when I see possible stirrings of a renewed cold war, when the trail demands walking sticks, when some from long ago begin to look ancestral, time-warped, when lost language returns—first comes recognition, then comes memory, come ghosts.

I make it normal.

ABOUT THE AUTHOR

Bian An, better known as *Ann Bennett Spence*, has a bicultural and biracial background. Her father was from a Republican family in the Boston area, and her mother from a distinguished Chinese family in Beijing. Her parents' marriage in 1940 was a news story, not a wedding announcement, so unusual in Boston was marriage between whites and Chinese immigrants still banned from citizenship. Bian An was their first-born.

In adulthood An(n) lived mainly in Cambridge MA and Palo Alto CA, and was married first to Michael Spence, and much later to Richard Bowers. She has three adult children. She was a managing director at a global investment firm, where she advised universities on governance and financial matters.

As a 2018 DCI Fellow at Stanford University, she researched her mother's decision to flee Japanese-occupied Beijing, for America. An(n) authored *Nancy Nianci: A Story of Wars,* a historical novel based on her findings. Currently her writing focuses on short stories, historical fiction, essays, and mystery, exploring race, family fracture, catastrophe—and renewal.

She lives in Exeter, NH and Boston, MA.

CPSIA information can be obtained
at www.ICGtesting.com
Printed in the USA
JSHW070217140223
37678JS00004B/4/J